Em Lou Productions presents

HIGH RIDIN'

BY JAMES HOGAN

This production officially opened at
the King's Head Theatre on
Tuesday 4 September 2018

CAST AND CREATIVE LIST

Stan   Tom Michael Blyth

Ronnie   Chi-Cho Tche

Ivy   Linda Beckett

Director Peter Darney
Designer Fin Redshaw
Lighting Designer Sherry Coenen
Sound Designer Nicola Chang
Assistant Director Alex Jackson
Stage Manager Lyndsey Bicker

CAST

TOM MICHAEL BLYTH

Recent theatre credits include: *The Father* (Bath Theatre Royal, West End & National Tour); *Hard Times* (Oldham Coliseum) for which he was nominated for Best Supporting Actor at the Manchester Theatre Awards; *The Hound of the Baskervilles* (Windsor Theatre Royal & National Tour); *John Bull's Other Island* (Shaw's Corner); *Twelfth Night* (Vienna English Theatre & International Tour); *Cadfael: The Virgin In The Ice* (National Tour); *The Duchess of Malfi* (New Diorama); *More Dead Girls* (Theatre 503); *Significant Other: Object of Affection* (Tristan Bates Theatre); *Off Cut Festival* (Riverside Studios); *The Importance of Being Earnest* (National Tour).

LINDA BECKETT

Linda Beckett was born and trained in Manchester. Theatre credits include: Mrs Kay in the stage premiere of Willy Russell's *Our Day Out*; Betty in his play *Breezeblock Park*; Maureen in Victoria Wood's *Talent*. Other roles include: Mrs Hardcastle in *She Stoops to Conquer* and the Widow Quinn in *Playboy of the Western World* which both toured internationally with Century Theatre. In 1974 Linda appeared in the original production of Willy Russell's *John, Paul, George, Ringo and Bert* (Liverpool Everyman and West End) which won the Evening Standard and London Theatre Critics awards for the best musical in 1974. Noted for her Elvis Presley impersonation in her one-woman show *Any Way You Want Me*, Linda also provided much of the fun as the earnest and rather dotty medium Madame Arcati in *Blithe Spirit* (Brewhouse Theatre, Taunton). Film credits include: Mike Leigh's *Bleak Moments*, *High Hopes* and his acclaimed *Secrets and Lies*. Television includes: Mike Leigh's *Hard Labour*; *Dummy*; *Vampires*; *Coronation Street*; *Extras*; Foggy's mum in *First of the Summer Wine*; *Some Mothers do Have 'Em*; *Bread*; *Joint Account*; *The Bill*; Rhona; *Doctors*.

CHI-CHO TCHE

Chi-Cho is a young actor from North London. He is thrilled to be making his professional stage debut in *High Ridin'*. He trained at the BRIT school of performing arts for two years. Whilst training he performed as Kevin in *Nini's Hair Salon* (New Wimbledon Theatre) and Sir Nathaniel in *Love's Labour's Lost* (RSC & Brighton Fringe Festival). He was also recently cast as Nick in the new Disney Channel original series *School Hacks*.

CREATIVE TEAM

DIRECTOR PETER DARNEY

Peter trained at the Royal Welsh College of Music and Drama. He wrote and directed the multi-award winning *5 Guys Chillin'* (King's Head Theatre/SoHo Playhouse Off-Broadway) which won Best LGBT Play 2017 at the Edinburgh Fringe and at the Doric Wilson Intercultural Dialogue Award at the Dublin International Gay Theatre festival. It has also been produced by The New Theatre Sydney and Kensington Hall Toronto and it is in early development as a film.

Other recent directing credits include: *Free and Proud* (King's Head Theatre/Theatre 503/Assembly Festival); *The Drag* (Arcola Theatre); *The Revengers Tragedy* (The Rose Playhouse); *Pinocchio* (Sutton Theatres); *Signal Failure* (SoHo Playhouse-Off Broadway 6 week run/The Underbelly, Edinburgh); *Kindness* (BBC Radio 4); *Frank Sent Me* (King's Head Theatre/ The Underbelly/Theatre 503/Soho Theatre, Best Play 2012 Writer's Avenue); *Githa* (St James Theatre, West End and York

Theatre Royal); *6 Degrees* (Soho Theatre: Main House); *Edward II* (The Rose Playhouse); *Mysterious Skin* (Gilded Balloon, The Drill Hall, Teacher's Club, Dublin); *Arden of Faversham* (The Rose Playhouse); *Beautiful thing* (BAC).

DESIGNER FIN REDSHAW

Fin Redshaw graduated with a first class BA Performance Design degree from The Royal Welsh College of Music & Drama in 2016. Her design works include: *In Arabia We'd All Be Kings* (Bute Theatre); *Mojo* (Richard Burton Theatre); *As It Occurs To Me* (Leicester Square Theatre); *Zero for the Young Dudes* (Sherman Theatre); *PLAY Takeover* (Bunker Theatre); *Islanders* (Soho Theatre); *Muswell Hill* (Linbury Studio Theatre) and *Love Me Now* (Tristan Bates Theatre). She has recently designed new musical *Pieces Of String* (Mercury Theatre, Colchester) after winning her category in the Linbury Prize 2017. Fin has also been nominated as Best Designer in The Stage Debut Awards 2018. In addition, Fin has worked as a design assistant to Rob Howell, Bob Crowley, Jonathan Fensom, Es Devlin and Ian McNeil.

LIGHTING DESIGNER SHERRY COENEN

Sherry has been lighting shows in the US and UK since graduating with a BFA in Lighting Design from the University of Miami in 2003. Shows include: *The Singing Mermaid* (Little Angel Theatre); *Izindava* (UK Tour); *This is How We Die* (UK Tour); *Africarmen* (UK Tour); *Cinderella* (Queen's Theatre, Hornchurch); *Skin Tight* (Park90); CELL (UK Tour); *Conquest of the South Pole* (Arcola); *These Trees are Made of Blood* (Arcola); *Brrr!* (UK Tour); *5 Guys Chillin'* (King's Head Theatre); *Anton Chekhov* (Hampstead Theatre).

SOUND DESIGNER NICOLA CHANG

Nicola has composed jazz, orchestral and electronic scores for independent films, theatre productions and commercial trailers across the UK, US and Asia. She has been playing percussion and piano for fifteen years, and has performed at the Royal Albert Hall and the Royal Festival Hall as a concert percussionist. Additionally, she is also a cast member of *STOMP!* (world tour) and a composer/Musical Director attached to Youth Music Theatre UK. Recent composition/ sound design credits include: *For Reasons That Remain Unclear...* (King's Head Theatre); *Free and Proud* (The King's Head Theatre/Edinburgh Assembly Festival); *Lost in Thought* (Underbelly); *Dangerous Giant Animals* (Underbelly); *The Free9* (NT Connections, National Theatre); *Finishing the Picture* (Finborough Theatre); *Nine Foot Nine* (Bunker Theatre); *Lord of the Flies* (Greenwich Theatre) and *Heretic Voices* (Arcola Theatre). To listen to some of her work, visit www.nicolatchang.com

ASSISTANT DIRECTOR ALEX JACKSON

Alex is a theatre director from the South West based in London. In March 2018, he joined the King's Head Theatre as a Trainee Resident Director and is excited to be working on *High Ridin'.* He is also Artistic Director of City of Light Theatre, a company with roots planted firmly in the South West's fertile soil. Previous credits as Director include *Henry: A Killer New Musical Workshop* (The Albany, Deptford); Michael Morpurgo's *Out of the Ashes* (The Bike Shed Theatre & South West Tour); *Jack and the Beanstalk* (South West Tour). As Associate Director: *Monmouth: The Westcountry Rebellion,* (Marine Theatre and South West Tour). As Assistant Director: *For Reasons That Remain Unclear...* (King's Head Theatre); *The Monstrum* (Marine Theatre).

STAGE MANAGER LYNDSEY BICKER

Lyndsey Bicker is a recent graduate from Buckinghamshire New University, she is a young actress and stage manager. Lyndsey has previously worked on Charles Gershman's *Free and Proud* (King's Head Theatre /Theatre 503) and Jackie Skarvellis' *James Dean is Dead! (Long Live James Dean)* (King's Head Theatre).

A Letter from the Artistic Director

Hello!

I'm thrilled to host James Hogan's brand new play *High Ridin'* and continue the King's Head Theatre's commitment to staging LGBTQI+ work and presenting the lives and relationships of the LGBTQI+ community on our stage. As the head of one of the UK's leading publishers, Oberon Books, James Hogan has been instrumental in championing the voices of young and emerging playwrights since 1986 so I am delighted that we can share one of his new plays as part of our 2018 Queer festival.

The King's Head Theatre has always been a home for ambitious programming and exciting emerging artists. Last year 116,151 audience members saw a show of ours: 44,607 at our 110-seater home on Upper Street and 71,544 on tour. At our home in Islington we had 774 performances last year of 95 different shows.

But we couldn't do any of this without your support. If you're already a supporter of the theatre thank you so much. If not would you consider signing up? You can become a Friend for just £25 a year. Every Friend and Supporter, as well as all the wonderful audience members who donate money in our bucket, is vital to ensuring we remain accessible for generations to come.

Thank you, enjoy your stay and we hope to see you again soon.

Adam

Adam Spreadbury-Maher
Artistic Director

Support the King's Head Theatre

The King's Head Theatre has always punched far above its weight. It is a bright star with a brighter future.

JOANNA LUMLEY

The King's Head Theatre is an ambitious, thriving producing house located in the heart of Islington. From the emerging companies and creatives we welcome to the 43,857 audience members we welcomed through our doors last year, people are at the heart of everything we do.

Famous for an unapologetically broad programme of work and an unwavering commitment to ethical employment on the fringe, the King's Head Theatre occupies a unique and critical place in the capital's theatre ecology.

Each year, the King's Head Theatre needs to raise £100,000 to keep producing and presenting ambitious work that supports, develops and values our artists, staff, audiences and alumni.

We hope you will join us on that journey by becoming one of our Supporters.

Memberships can be purchased on our website at **kingsheadtheatre.com**, in person at the box office or by telephoning **020 7226 8561**

For further information or to discuss bespoke packages to suit you, please contact Alan on friends@kingsheadtheatre.com

KEY TO THE STAGE DOOR from £150 per year

Priority Booking Period
Exchange and reserve tickets at no extra cost
'KHT Insights' email with production news and announcements ahead of the press
Invitations to Supporters' Nights including private pre-show discussions
Acknowledgement in our published playtexts and programmes
How this gift might help: £275 pays an actor's wages for one week

KEY TO THE DRESSING ROOM from £500 per year

All membership benefits offered with Key to the Stage Door plus:
Invitation to annual 'Behind the Scenes Breakfast' to hear the Artistic Director share upcoming
plans for the King's Head Theatre.
Personal booking via the Development Manager
How this gift might help: £500 pays for all the costumes for one of our operas

KEY TO THE KING'S HEAD THEATRE from £1000 per year

All membership benefits offered with Key to the Dressing Room plus:
Invitation once a year to breakfast with the Executive Director.
Opportunity to book house seats to sold out shows
How this gift might help: £1,375 supports the Director for one production

ARTISTIC DIRECTOR'S CIRCLE from £2,500 per year

All membership benefits offered with Key to the King's Head Theatre plus:
Playtext signed by the company for each production attended
Invitation to lunch with the Artistic Director once a year
Opportunity to be given a backstage tour of the theatre for you and up to 5 guests finishing
with drinks on the King's Head Theatre's stage
How this gift might help: £2,500 pays for the set design for one of our plays

AMBASSADOR from £5,000 per year

An exclusive chance to be a truly integral part of the life of the King's Head Theatre.
All of the benefits of Artistic Director's Circle plus invitations to our Press Nights and post-show
parties and the chance to create additional bespoke benefits suited to your interests.
How this gift might help: £5,775 pays for the actors during the rehearsal period of a show

King's Head Theatre

The King's Head Theatre is 47 years old, here are just a few of the highlights of our journey so far...

1970
Dan Crawford founds the first pub theatre in London since Shakespeare's day and the King's Head Theatre is born.

1983
A revival of *Mr Cinders*, starring Joanna Lumley, opens at the King's Head Theatre before transferring to the West End. It goes on to run for 527 performances.

1986
Maureen Lipman stars in the Olivier Award nominated *Wonderful Town* at the King's Head Theatre.

1988
Premier of Tom Stoppard's *Artist Descending a Staircase* opens at the King's Head Theatre before transferring to Broadway.

1991
Steven Berkoff directs and stars in the UK premiere of *Kvetch* at the King's Head Theatre.

1992
Trainee Resident Directors Scheme wins Royal Anniversary Trust Award.

2010
Opera Up Close, founded by Adam Spreadbury-Maher and Robin Norton-Hale become resident company for 4 years.

2011
La bohème wins the Olivier Award for Best New Opera Performance.

2015
King's Head Theatre forms a new charity to secure the future of the theatre.

2015
Shock Treatment, the sequel to *Rocky Horror Show*, premiers at the King's Head Theatre and *Trainspotting* is first performed at the King's Head Theatre – in May 2017 it hit its 600th performance.

2016
43,857 audience members see a show at our London home - our highest footfall ever.

2018
La bohème is nominated for the Olivier Award for Best New Opera Production following a 5 week run at Trafalgar Studios.

2020
King's Head Theatre moves to its new permanent home in Islington Square securing the future of the venue for generations to come.

HIGH RIDIN'

by James Hogan

⅃SAMUEL FRENCH⅃

samuelfrench.co.uk

FOR AMATEUR PRODUCTION ENQUIRIES

UNITED KINGDOM AND WORLD
EXCLUDING NORTH AMERICA
plays@samuelfrench.co.uk
020 7255 4302/01

Each title is subject to availability from Samuel French,
depending upon country of performance.

THINKING ABOUT PERFORMING A SHOW?

There are thousands of plays and musicals available to perform from Samuel French right now, and applying for a licence is easier and more affordable than you might think

From classic plays to brand new musicals, from monologues to epic dramas, there are shows for everyone.

Plays and musicals are protected by copyright law, so if you want to perform them, the first thing you'll need is a licence. This simple process helps support the playwright by ensuring they get paid for their work and means that you'll have the documents you need to stage the show in public.

Not all our shows are available to perform all the time, so it's important to check and apply for a licence before you start rehearsals or commit to doing the show.

LEARN MORE & FIND THOUSANDS OF SHOWS

Browse our full range of plays and musicals, and find out more about how to license a show
www.samuelfrench.co.uk/perform

Talk to the friendly experts in our Licensing team for advice on choosing a show and help with licensing
plays@samuelfrench.co.uk   020 7387 9373

Acting Editions

BORN TO PERFORM

Playscripts designed from the ground up to work the way you do in rehearsal, performance and study

---

Larger, clearer text for easier reading

Wider margins for notes

Performance features such as character and props lists, sound and lighting cues, and more

---

+ CHOOSE A SIZE AND STYLE TO SUIT YOU

  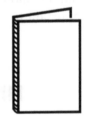

STANDARD EDITION	**SPIRAL-BOUND EDITION**	**LARGE EDITION**
Our regular paperback book at our regular size	The same size as the Standard Edition, but with a sturdy, easy-to-fold, easy-to-hold spiral-bound spine	A4 size and spiral bound, with larger text and a blank page for notes opposite every page of text – perfect for technical and directing use

Other plays by JAMES HOGAN
published and licensed by Samuel French

Ivy and Joan

FIND PERFECT PLAYS TO PERFORM AT
www.samuelfrench.co.uk/perform

ABOUT THE AUTHOR

James Hogan's plays include *Peacefully in his Sleep* (Gate Theatre 1978); *The Guest Room* (Not the RSC Festival and Old Red Lion Theatre 1986); *Venetian Gold* (Cockpit Theatre London, Edinburgh Festival, King's Head Islington 1991); *Trotsky and Our Ernie* (Cockpit 1990); *Ivy & Joan* (Print Room 2014, Jermyn Street Theatre 2016).

James is the founder publisher of the theatre publishers Oberon Books. He has been a journalist/editor in the business sector and published several titles including The European Marketplace (Macmillan).

Academic activities include Lecturer in Theatre Studies (London Guildhall University), Honorary Fellow of the Royal College of Art.

AUTHOR'S NOTE

Although the location is a house on the West Pennine Moors, the characters are rooted in Lancashire working class urban culture. They are not farmers. One can imagine that the family set up the guest house years ago but, due to human failings and traumatic events the business failed. STAN, now forty five inherits this relic from a father he believed was hostile to his queer lifestyle.

STAN is a bluff ex security guard who has done time in prison. He needs to make a new start. He picks up RONNIE who needs a lift to Blackpool but veers off the motorway to the house on the moors. RONNIE has smoked the lethal drug, Spice, and slumped in the passenger seat. STAN must avoid being caught with him. Disillusioned with his family, RONNIE is also seeking a new life. So, the two men have each made a conscious decision to start afresh. Aunt IVY is a more instinctive being. Straight-laced, religious and firmly opposed to homosexuality. But she too is about to change. Her journey is more inwardly driven. So, the theme is forgiveness which leads to redemption.

NOTES ON THE PLOT

The key moments in the plot occur when:

STAN discovers IVY stealing valuable items from the house. IVY makes away with a precious painting while STAN is distracted by RONNIE. IVY returns the painting on the orders of her offstage husband, Derrick.

IVY hands over a letter written by STAN's father which bequeaths the house to him. She had thrown it away, but husband Derrick retrieves it. She must now confess and ask for forgiveness.

RONNIE, focussed on the new job in Blackpool, suddenly absconds, despite his drugged hangover. This sparks a confrontation as IVY persuades STAN not to go after him.

But here is the soul of the drama – STAN is desolate and likely to crumble. Now reaching middle-age, he faces a stark choice. A lonely life, cruising the M6 for queer youths, or will he settle down and rebuild the guest house business? He isn't emotionally equipped to do that alone. He is grieving for **RONNIE** who has captured his heart.

All is not lost. There is a surprise in store. **IVY** reappears. She herself has found **RONNIE** sheltering from the storm. She knows that **RONNIE** is the last hope to redeem the family business. A wise old hand, she plants **RONNIE** back in the house, hoping that he will seize the opportunity to join the family.

RONNIE, a canny little guy with an eye to business gets it, as they say. The play ends with **STAN** joyfully hopeful for a better future – as indeed they all are. The promise of two dogs is the bait for **RONNIE**. The rollercoaster ride on Blackpool pleasure Beach underlines the risks ahead and the race into the unknown.

When it comes to staging, the gloomy legacy of bereavement and decline could be rooted in the design of the dusty Victorian lounge in which the action takes place. At the beginning there is no electricity, but the supply is restored later. Offstage Derrick again, acting as a Deus ex Machina behind the scenes. Therefore, in design terms, the atmosphere changes from gloomy to bright.

The storm interlude can be achieved by sound. But if a production is technically ambitious a deluge can be projected. The same applies to the rollercoaster ride. Sound will do. Perhaps a strobe effect as **STAN** and **RONNIE** sit side by side on the chaise longue (or sofa).

MUSIC USE NOTE

Licensees are solely responsible for obtaining formal written permission from copyright owners to use copyrighted music in the performance of this play and are strongly cautioned to do so. If no such permission is obtained by the licensee, then the licensee must use only original music that the licensee owns and controls. Licensees are solely responsible and liable for all music clearances and shall indemnify the copyright owners of the play(s) and their licensing agent, Samuel French, against any costs, expenses, losses and liabilities arising from the use of music by licensees. Please contact the appropriate music licensing authority in your territory for the rights to any incidental music.

IMPORTANT BILLING AND CREDIT REQUIREMENTS

If you have obtained performance rights to this title, please refer to your licensing agreement for important billing and credit requirements.

FIRST PERFORMANCE INFO

High Ridin' was first performed at the King's Head Theatre,
London on 4th September 2018 with the following cast:

Stan   Tom Michael Blyth

Ronnie   Chi-Cho Tche

Ivy   Linda Beckett

Director Peter Darney
Designer Fin Redshaw
Lighting Designer Sherry Coenen
Sound Designer Nicola Chang
Assistant Director Alex Jackson
Stage Manager Lyndsey Bicker

CHARACTERS

STAN, aged forty-five, is a loner but not a happy one. He left home after his father discovered he was queer, took a job in night security and ended up in prison for small-time drug dealing. He has also lost his best pal, his dog (Mastiff). With a chip on his shoulder, his demeanour is "straight" brutal working class. Tough and gruff at first, his wounded emotions surface later in the play.

IVY, aged seventy-plus. Of the old school. At first homophobic and vociferously disapproving of Stan and his lifestyle. Her religious convictions are only skin deep. She's not above stealing from a dead man's house, items which she conveniently regards as her entitlement. It is her offstage husband, Derrick, who represents a conscience turns the tables. Towards the end of the play the latent warmth in her character is re-awakened. She wants the family guest house restored and takes the action needed to make it happen.

RONNIE, aged eighteen. A hard-nosed working-class teenager raised in South London against a background of a multicultural melting pot of gangs and estate life. But Ronnie has charm, and this doesn't fit with his coarse background. Neither does his background fit with being queer. Pluckily, he has decided to go it alone, as so many young queer men do. His catering qualification is his only hope for a new job far away in Blackpool. The one emotional pull towards home is also a dog, the Staffie he pines for which he had to leave behind.

SETTING

The action takes place in a run-down guest house on the Lancashire Moors.

Scene One

Stan's House

*A bankrupted country guest house on the Lancashire
Moors. The lounge, with a bay window. There is a vintage
framed painting of a boat on a lake on the wall, small
enough to carry.*

IVY *(70) is stashing knick-knacks and antiques into a
holdall as best she can using a walking stick for support,
then she turns to the painting.*

STAN *(42) quietly appears and stands in the doorway.
He has two bags of shopping. He watches* IVY *and videos
her on his mobile.*

IVY *leans her walking stick on the chaise longue so that
she can take the painting off the wall.*

STAN Enjoying yourself, Ivy?

IVY Oh!

STAN Am I interruptin' something?

IVY When did *you* get here?

STAN Just in time obviously.

IVY They told us next week.

STAN Oh, did they. Her Majesty's holiday camp, the admin's
worse than the food, and that's saying something. *(Puts the
shopping down)* Now tell me, what the fuck d'you think
you're doin'?

IVY There's no need for bad language.

STAN Game of friendly burglars, is it? Yes? No? You're the gang boss. Derrick's the wheelsman in the getaway car. I play the detective come to arrest you. Your idea of a welcome home party.

IVY Stop acting the goat. Not everything in this house is yours.

STAN Yes it is. I am the sole inheritant.

IVY If you mean beneficiary...

STAN Whatever the law says. Look at it, bags of loot and more in the fuckin' car.

IVY I refuse to discuss any of this until you modify your language.

STAN What! No swearing in my own fuckin' house!

IVY Worse than ever. It's disgusting. Effing this, effing that. I'm stunned the way you speak to me.

STAN Come off it, Ivy. They couldn't stun you in the electric chair. Stick to the point. That car is so stuffed with antiques, an Aladdin's cave on wheels, it's almost a professional job.

IVY They're not antiques.

STAN It's not a car boot sale neither. Talk about takin' liberties. Ivy Avarice, but I never thought you'd sink *this* low. You're stripping the house bare. What's next? The wallpaper? Don't bother. It's holding up the building.

IVY Have y'done? Have y'done with your comedy turn?

STAN Except I don't think it's funny. It's polite to ask if you want things. Here's me teaching the elderly good manners. What's the world coming to?

IVY If you've quite finished... I was born in this house. I'm entitled to what's mine.

STAN Nothing's yours. You left when? Thirty years ago to marry a church warden. Now he's your accomplice. I've just told him. He didn't like it and shut the car window in my face.

IVY Leave Derrick out of it.

STAN For the record, you're not entitled to enter the building. No one is.

IVY Who says so?

STAN It's private property.

IVY Derrick and I are family. Or have you forgotten?

STAN Private property with public access? How d'you work that out? *(Beat)* Right. From now on, no more sundry folk to wander in and out as they please. Suppose I fetch up in your house when it suits me to? I'd like to hear what *you* say. You'd swear like a fuckin' brickie!

IVY I doubt it.

STAN Go on, say "fuck" to please me. It won't give you throat cancer.

IVY You don't change, do you, Stan.

STAN I can't get through to you, can I? You're committing a crime. Think of the shame on Facebook. Here's the video. *(Shows her his phone)*

IVY You don't frighten me. I was born in this house.

STAN I was born in Blackpool Victoria Hospital, but I don't own the furniture.

IVY *(scoffs)* Huh!

STAN This evidence on video, I could show this to the police and you would definiely be arrested. Headline "The geriatric Bonnie and Clyde raid country houses". Aunty Ivy – dear – I'm trying to make it clear that Dad's death changes everything.

IVY My brother's death. Talk about shame? You brought shame on the whole family.

STAN There's shame you see and shame you don't. How does it go? Derrick came home early to find you in your parlour with a six-foot six brickie. Dad said you were a right little tart in those days. Is it true you wore stilettoes on the beach? OK, we won't go there.

IVY Nothing you go to prison for! *(Points to the holdall)* Don't I own anything? These few things and what your dad said I could take!

STAN Where's Bobby? *(Pause)* Silence like thunder. I'll try again. Where's Bobby?

IVY Don't ask me. I had nothing to do with it.

STAN Nothing to do with what?

IVY Your dad couldn't look after it any more. I don't *know* what he did with it.

STAN "It"? Don't like the sound of that. "It". Dad did nothing with him? The last letter I got said Bobby was a happy dog.

IVY Don't start on me, Stan. Ask Derrick. I'm not involved...

IVY *puts the picturegraph in the holdall.*

STAN When you know about things, you *are* involved. The Good Samaritan, the most forgotten parable of all. Come on, Ivy, Mastiffs don't disappear into thin air. Or was he let loose on the moors to fend for'isself?

IVY Stan, I...

STAN See, you *do* know.

IVY Oh, for God's sake!

STAN I'm not letting this one go, Ivy. If Bobby's been put down, there'll be hell to play.

IVY There's hell to play now. I told you! I know nothing about it. Kennels, I suppose! That's where dogs go, isn't it?

STAN Kennels. Which kennels?

IVY I don't know.

STAN I'll find out. Google local kennels. *(Starts to Google)*

IVY That won't get you anywhere.

STAN Why not?

IVY Stan, be reasonable for once. You're only upsetting yourself.

STAN Upset am I? That says it all. *(Puts his phone away)* Go on, fuck off with the gear and don't come back.

IVY Stan, don't be childish. It was for the best.

STAN Best for who?

Pause. He grieves for Bobby.

IVY There is a dog afterlife. D'you remember Norma Fenton down the lane? She saw her dog in the garden three days after it died.

STAN *(Puts on a brave face)* Well! Nice to see the village shop's still goin' strong. No candles though. I said "What 'appens in a power cut, apart from the birth-rate goes up?"

He tries to turn on a side lamp. No power.

So, who told them to disconnect?

IVY There's no point in paying...

STAN *You* did. But you never thought to empty the fridge, did you? How long's that been? Fur-coated bacon.

IVY The prodigal son returns, no warning, wants everything ticketyboo, all spic and span, as if nothing's happened.

STAN Or d'you mean the abomination returns?

IVY I'm not listening.

STAN Or am I still the runt in a litter of one. If Dad'd been well enough to make a will...

IVY Here we go! One word in the heat of the moment. He didn't mean it.

STAN How do you know he didn't mean it? Depends who poisoned his mind. I think he did mean it.

IVY I know he didn't. Five minutes in the house and you bring that up. What for? To cause trouble like you always do.

STAN The runt in a litter of one? How can anyone forget that?

IVY Stan, why can't we have a *nice* conversation?

STAN I'm an abomination, the Bible says so.

IVY You believed in the Bible once. What went wrong?

STAN I read it. The bits they made movies of. I admit I read it more for effect like, while my cell-mate's whacking one off to underwear adverts.

IVY Whacking?

STAN Solves the Rubik's Cube in the dark. How about that? *(Beat. She doesn't get it)* His porn was confiscated. Used his imagination.

IVY You want to provoke me, but I haven't got the time.

IVY *is determined to leave with the stolen goods.* STAN *blocks her leaving.*

Let me go please.

STAN Hard as brass tacks. Don't you read me? This doesn't belong to you. Show me what you've got. *(He takes the holdall off her)*

IVY This is harassment. I'm not putting up with it.

STAN *looks inside the holdall. He takes the photograph out.*

STAN All yours? Toby jugs. Grandad's medals. What the fuckin' fuck d'you think you're doing? These are my grandad's medals!

IVY My brother's medals.

STAN *puts the medals on the coffee table and hangs the photograph back on the wall.*

STAN The medals! I'm flabber-fuckin'- gasted. Poor Dad must be turning in his grave.

IVY He was cremated.

STAN He'd be turning in his grave if he had one. Where's his ashes then?

IVY We'll have a proper talk when you're in a better mood. As regards, the contents of the house, as family, we're entitled to a few mementos. Derrick and I surmised what's ours and...

STAN So, dear Uncle Derrick put you up to this? How? Did he switch his other brain cell on?

IVY Derrick knows the law.

STAN Knows the law? Derrick can't cope with a fuckin' parkin' ticket. *(Re the picture)* I want this. The annual boat ride on Lake Windermere. How many summers are in this picture? This room without this picture is like a picnic without scenery. You can't just nab other people's memories.

IVY We *all* went on that boat together.

STAN Dad'd never part with it. He had an eye for a bargain watching the Antiques Roadshow. Look, the dining room clock! This is Victorian.

IVY It's repro y'silly sod, ormulu. Look, Stan, you've got the house. Why be so stingy?

STAN Me stingy? You wouldn't breathe out if you didn't have to.

IVY *fastens the holdall.*

Fuck off. Don't expect a Christmas card.

IVY That's up to you. Right, so we get these, you get the picture. Are we agreed?

STAN What about the keys? Don't bother. I'll change the locks. Insurance, the small print. You know what they're like. A mate o' mine got no compensation cos his *dog* didn't bark. My Bobby though; Bobby had a bark like a sonic boom. I will hear that bark in my head for the rest of my days? That's the afterlife.

IVY *(competing for the sentiment stakes)* It wasn't easy for us, Stan. He was ill for a long time. Dementia, they're gone before they go. I took care of him, and at the end all the formalities, hospital, care home, the funeral. Then we had to shut down the business. We had no choice. There were no visitors anyway. Try it some time; accountants, solicitors... Where were you, the only son?

STAN Don't blame me. Blame the vodka. The old sod was an indoor wino.

STAN *is looking out of the window with his back to her.*

IVY All right, I'm goin'. I will say one thing though...

STAN Another one thing?

IVY It took the miracle of the universe to put you on God's Earth. D'you think you've done your best?

STAN Have you? He was living knee deep in dirt.

IVY Social services sent a home help. Your dad wouldn't let him in. We won't say why. And at my age on my knees with a scrubbing brush? I can't do it.

STAN There's enough germs in that kitchen to start a new planet. The fridge is contaminated, mouldy tins, stinking trash bin, and for good measure, a dead mouse in a pan of gravy.

IVY It's a potato.

STAN And you left it there? Christ, what a way to go, drowned in Bisto.

IVY It's not a mouse! It's a potato in oxtail soup.

STAN You didn't dispose of it?

IVY I've been overwhelmed. Ambulance, paramedics, the dog...

She realises she has slipped up mentioning the dog.

You don't know the full story. You wouldn't listen if I told you.

STAN *(cold)* The dog I would. Bobby had a soul, more than some people I know.

IVY Especially when he wanted a biscuit. Stop tormenting me about the damn dog!

STAN Quiet please. I've got a visitor upstairs...

IVY The dog was your responsibility! Why didn't you think of that before...

STAN Excuse me. *(Points upstairs)* My visitor.

IVY *(stern)* I remember when we had lots of visitors. The best guest house in the whole district.

STAN I'm selling up.

IVY The life you lead, it's just as well.

RONNIE *(offstage, upstairs)* STAN!

STAN Now what.

> STAN *rushes to the door.*

IVY Who's that?

STAN Mind your own business.

RONNIE Stan! Stan!

> STAN *exits to go upstairs.* IVY *scurries to the door and calls after him.*

IVY You don't know what it was like here! No bloody idea! Waltzing back in like the lord of the manor!

> IVY *dumps the keys on the table. On the spur of the moment, she steals the picturegraph and tucks it away in the holdall.*

> IVY *exits.*

End of Scene One

Scene Two

RONNIE is lying on the chaise longue. He is wearing only his boxer shorts and white socks.

IVY's walking stick is still propped against the chaise longue.

There is a pair of folding steps near the window.

STAN enters carrying a pair of jeans, t-shirt, socks, trainers, and a glass of water. He dumps the clothes and stands near RONNIE holding the glass. He waits.

STAN Water. You're dehydrated.

He puts the water down. He feels RONNIE's temperature and pulse.

Eighty. Fast as a pixie's wank. It's a known fact, if you don't drink enough fluid, your dick shrinks.

RONNIE sits up slowly.

Works every time. How d'you feel?

RONNIE Chronic. Has she gone?

STAN Scarpered. *(Points to the walking stick)* But she left her broomstick behind. Last night, fright of my life, sonny boy, I thought you were dead. I carried you upstairs in a coma. If you wanna kill yourself, not in my house please, you'll overstay your welcome.

RONNIE I'm OK.

STAN No, you're not. You OD'd. How do I explain to paramedics? A teenage boy collapsed in my house. I have some knowledge of these things, I've been monitoring the situation.

RONNIE I never OD.

STAN What is it? Crack? Meth? Junk?

RONNIE A spliff.

STAN What was in it? I never saw you smokin'. Where? Behind the shed like a schoolboy?

RONNIE Respect. I'm eighteen, not fifteen.

STAN I reckon it's Spice. Drink this for fuck's sake. Even a car needs water. You're a human being... I think.

RONNIE How old are you? Over forty.

STAN Only in daylight. Don't be cheeky.

RONNIE Got any paracetamol?

STAN No way. Bad for your kidneys.

RONNIE Paracetamol! I've got a headache.

STAN I wouldn't trust you with M&Ms. Can you stand up? Show me. Ronnie.

RONNIE Chill. I'm like thinkin' en I, where we was...

STAN You don't remember me? So, am I a complete stranger to you? Go back to the beginning. You came here in my car!

RONNIE I know, the motorway.

STAN D'you know where you are at the moment?

RONNIE (looks around) The Psycho house?

STAN No. This is not the Bates Motel. Welcome to the West Pennine Moors. An area of outstanding natural beauty. Cycling, walking, bird watching.

RONNIE Where the Moors Murders were?

STAN That's Saddleworth, the other way. Sixty years ago. How do you know that?

RONNIE Netflix.

STAN Yeah, well we don't talk about the Moors Murders. It affects property values. D'you still feel sick? You puked all over the bathroom.

RONNIE D'you bring all the boys here?

STAN My dad died recently. He left me the house. You're the first.

RONNIE Creepy though, ennit? Like it's haunted. If I go down
the cellar, what will I see? Dead boys in the freezer?

STAN Do I look like a killer?

RONNIE Killers don't look like killers. They're like you and
me. Mostly you.

STAN Well, I hate to disappoint you. I'm not Norman Bates.
This is not the Psycho house.

RONNIE You act geeky though.

STAN Geeky?

RONNIE Nervy. Yeah, just *like* Norman Bates.

STAN If I was like Norman Bates, I'd be digging your grave by
now. What exactly d'you mean by geeky? (STAN *Googles*)

RONNIE OK, so you're a diamond geezer, no worries. (*A sudden
turn for the worse*) Help me out, mister! I'm seein' inside
my brain.

STAN Is there anything there? D'you know what Spice actually
does to your brain? It fucks you up forever.

RONNIE OK, don't go off on one.

STAN Why d'you think they call it the zombie drug? It changes
how you think, or even if you ever think again. It's not like
weed. On Spice you go to hell or Fairyland, and maybe you
don't come back. A bad trip goes on for days. Flashbacks,
the whole fuckin' psychodynamic showcase.

RONNIE No worries, mate. When you're dead you don't know
you're dead.

STAN I'm not taking you anywhere till I know you're sober.
(*Reading his mobile*) "Geek: a socially awkward person, a
person obsessed with technology, a carnival performer of

bizarre acts like swallowing live frogs". I could be offended by that.

RONNIE You're out of your box. Eatin' live frogs for fuck's sake.

STAN It's on Google, look. *(Shows him the Google entry)*

RONNIE Hold on. I'm thinkin' timewise, like where I'm due to be now. Where's my watch?

STAN Bedside table. Show me your eyes.

STAN *stoops to look.*

RONNIE Oh, are we back on? I need my toothbrush.

STAN Bloodshot. *(Picks up the glass of water)* Come on, be a good boy, drink this.

RONNIE What is it?

STAN Tap water.

RONNIE That's a fuckin' aquarium. Fish and shit. What amoebas is in there? Look, see what I'm sayin'? Amoebas. Infection.

STAN *puts the water down.*

STAN The junk you put in your body and you complain about the water?

RONNIE Nobody drinks that! Amoebas are parasites.

STAN I've got orange juice. Fresh from the shop. *(Heads for the door to get it)*

RONNIE Where d'you keep it? That dirty fridge?

STAN I give up. I need you outa here. I've got things to do before dark.

RONNIE Got any coke?

STAN Which kind? No to both.

RONNIE You know what I mean. Coke! Lemonade! Wipe the top clean first. Hygiene.

STAN Look who's talkin'. Just now you pissed out the window.

RONNIE Yeah, for good hygiene. The toilet don't flush. I don't piss on your jobbies.

STAN Sorry, I didn't know. It's not the only toilet we have. All bedrooms ensuite like any decent guest house. Jesus, if one Spice roll-up sends you this far under...

RONNIE Just...chill. Chill. Stop vexing me.

STAN Where d'you get the stuff? Those scally lads back there? The games arcade. I suppose you're all innocently shooting down Martians.

RONNIE Space mutants.

STAN Space mutants. Pardon me.

RONNIE On camera? Nobody's that dumb. That whole place is on camera. You know that. Why're you even askin'?

STAN You're totally zoned out in my car! Crashed out like a corpse and nearly hanged yourself on the seat belt. There's cameras all up the M6 as well. Think about that. Face recognition. Me with a zombie in the passenger seat. By now my picture's gone viral in every police station in Lancashire, Yorkshire, Merseyside, Greater Manchester and Cheshire. *(Beat)* Why do I always forget Derbyshire?

RONNIE You're paranoid ennit? By the way, soldier, did we fuck?

STAN No. I feel differently now. You sleep around. Boys like you, no thank you, not even with double condoms, rubber gloves and a face mask.

RONNIE I need a shag, not surgery. You're sayin' I'm a slut and you don't even know me.

STAN You don't remember my name.

RONNIE If we're *not* gonna fuck, this is kidnapping.

STAN I may have saved your life.

RONNIE Bullshit! Where's the ambulance? You gave me a bed to die in. Big of you but it ain't savin' my life.

STAN Ronnie, how do I explain a teenage runaway in a coma?

RONNIE I'm not a runaway. I'm my own person. I make my own decisions.

STAN The wrong ones obviously.

RONNIE Don't act like you're in church. You're a badman.

STAN That makes two of us. Cruising the M6 at night.

RONNIE Not me. Was I cruisin'? You're the prowler. Down my end I don't go out nights. It ain't safe. Only with the dog, daytime. That's the worst thing about leaving home.

STAN What.

RONNIE My dog. I can't stop thinkin' about her. I see her face all the time, waiting for me. One day soon I *will* go back for her.

STAN If you miss your dog, why did you leave?

RONNIE Money. Lost my job, just for arguing what's right. Zero hours, minimum wage. It's a fuckin' joke. Look, I need a lift to Blackpool, not sittin' ere talkin' to you.

STAN I'm trying to be helpful.

RONNIE Mind games, I don't need it. I'm fit. Are *you* ready to go?

STAN Let me put you on a train to London.

RONNIE When'd I say go home? I don't wanna go home. I'm due in Blackpool. My mate Karl's expecting me.

STAN What about your dog then?

RONNIE I can't talk to you, can I. I say one thing, you say another.

STAN I like dogs! What sort of dog?

RONNIE Staffie. I wish I'd hadn't said it now.

STAN What's its name?

RONNIE Brindle! She's brindle colour.

STAN So you *call* her Brindle.

RONNIE Fuck me, you're clever.

STAN Just testing. You're perking up, good. But I wanna see you walk, walk about the room.

RONNIE (not sure) Gimme a minute. I was sleepin' on my leg. (Rubs his leg)

STAN Can you feel it?

RONNIE Yeah. I can feel it.

STAN Let's hope it isn't a stroke. Can you move it?

RONNIE Yep. (Moves his leg)

STAN Are you kidding me?

RONNIE That movement is not a lie.

STAN Rest up. I've got one more thing to do.

STAN mounts the steps near the window to check the locks.

RONNIE At my age you don't get strokes.

STAN I beg to differ.

RONNIE Don't own me. I know. When you stop playing Spiderman maybe we can move on. I'm linkin' with Karl for a reason.

STAN It's about an hour up the M6/M55, depending on the weekend traffic.

RONNIE I can drive y'know. (Grins. He doesn't mean it)

STAN High as a demented skylark? No you fuckin' can't.

RONNIE You get used to it, blue traffic lights. Nah, I'm 'avin' a laugh. Come on, man. What yer doin' up there?

STAN Not playing Spiderman. The lock's buggered. It's an open invitation.

RONNIE Spiderman's hot. Spiderman porn is. Google images, you don't have to pay. It's amazing. My dad looks at it. Children should block adult content on parent's computers.

STAN *comes down off the steps.*

STAN I'm not dressing up as Spiderman. Have you got any money? Or is that a silly question?

RONNIE Yeah. I need to eat.

STAN You spent it all on drugs.

RONNIE I don't have no chance in this place cuz you bad mind me every time.

STAN I bought some doughnuts.

RONNIE Where d'you put them?

STAN The kitchen. Clean doughnuts in a clean packet in a clean bag.

RONNIE So where's the bag? You got maggots in the fridge, mister.

STAN Maggots he says. White rice actually. Ivy must have left it there.

RONNIE Rice don't move.

STAN It does if you're hallucinating. This is not a good sign, mate. You're still trippin'

RONNIE Also a cockroach in the sink.

STAN Oh, giveover. There's no cockroaches. You know what you are? You're a germaphobe.

RONNIE I know what a cockroach is. I work in takeaways. The boss man chef stamps on cockroaches. His idea of pest control. He's not a proper chef though, just a franchisee with a fuckin' fryin' pan. I told him, "Don't you know you're breakin' the hygiene laws?" I was at catering college. I know! He don't know shit. I got two GCSEs.

STAN What in? Wankin 'n' chillin?

RONNIE *stands up and begins to get dressed.*

Can I ask about your parents? Do they know where you are?

RONNIE Yeah, that's what's goin' on with me right now, family.

STAN D'you wanna tell me?

RONNIE My business. I don't know you.

STAN Fair enough.

STAN *spots the space on the wall where the picture was hanging.*

The wicked cow. She's nicked my dad's picture!

RONNIE You mean that old woman? Who was she?

STAN My Aunty Ivy. Fuckin' thieving bitch.

RONNIE The way she looked at me like I'm a criminal, accusin'. You're a criminal don't make me one, does it? Did you see her?

STAN How d'you know about me?

RONNIE Why are you so scared of the police?

STAN *(beat)* So what's the deal with *your* family?

RONNIE No more questions. Let's go.

STAN Are *you* in trouble with the law?

RONNIE More questions. You gonna waterboard me?

RONNIE *puts his trainers on.*

Talk about better things, like y'got a good dick. *(Grin)*

STAN Thanks. I'm Stan, by the way, the man attached to it.

RONNIE Pleased to meet you, Stan. *(Smiling)* You look trim fit, pity you're a wasteman.

STAN What's a wasteman?

RONNIE What it says. Fuckin' useless. So why did we link in the first place? See what I'm sayin'? *(Sexy)* So what're we gonna do about this, Stan? You and me.

STAN Sorry, I like humans, not zombies.

RONNIE Now, Stan, that ain't nice. But I know what your beef
is, the drugs scene. Listen, this Spice thing. To tell you the
truth, I thought it was high grade weed. I'm in this club
watchin' some crazy hip-hop whirly boy spin on his head,
like a hundred spins non-stop. Competition winner.

STAN Do his brains fly out of his ears?

RONNIE No, listen please. This camp batty boy in pink shorts
comes up to me. Gives me a spliff. But I didn't smoke it
there. I went back on the road.

STAN Givin' you a taster. Trying to get you hooked. Which club?

RONNIE (*frustrated, evasive*) Manchester. I was in Manchester.
I don't know Manchester! Truck driver took a wrong turning.
So I end up in the middle of the city.

STAN You can't take a wrong turning off the M6 unless you
drive backwards.

RONNIE He forgot me in the back of the truck.

STAN D'you expect me you believe this tale?

RONNIE That's the God's honest truth.

STAN Ronnie, butter wouldn't melt in your mouth. It wouldn't
melt if it slid right through you and dropped out your arse.
You could be a dealer sat right here in my house. I don't
wanna go back to prison. Not because I don't like the fuckin'
food! (*Beat*) I have bad memories about prison.

RONNIE I don't know how you can say this to me. I'm being
honest with you. I'm telling you what happened.

STAN Manchester, hip hop, wrong turning, disco, batty boy,
pink shorts, a spliff, high grade weed. Too much detail,
Ronnie. It's what bad liars always do, dress up their lies.
I know the game. You're right. I've been in trouble myself.

RONNIE What kind of trouble?

STAN Wait 'til we're on the road. We'll have a coffee on the motorway,

RONNIE Hey, will you buy me an all-day breakfast?

STAN If there's time.

RONNIE You payin'?

STAN *(sighs like "here we go")* Blackpool, Hades-on-Sea, Zombieville.

RONNIE They got rollercoasters, don't they. Ten rollercoasters. The Big One's lit, two hundred and twenty-five feet high, eighty-five miles an hour. Karl and me, we're goin' there tonight, the Pleasure Beach. D'you wanna join in? It's late night fireworks night.

STAN Trippin' I suppose. Where y'stayin', a squat house? Wouldn't surprise me.

RONNIE There you go again. No respect. Karl works in a big hotel. He's gonna sneak me into staff quarters. Or I sleep under a pier.

STAN The tide comes in.

RONNIE I need this new job. He's got me an interview. Four o'clock. Time to go. Don't fuck me up.

STAN Too late, kid. You've lost the job. Spaced out like this you lose all sense of time.

RONNIE So *what's* the time?

STAN Three o'clock. We won't make it.

RONNIE You coulda woke me.

STAN I tried all morning. Look, it's peak season, there's plenty of jobs. Just walk down the front and look. You've got experience.

RONNIE *(pause)* Yeah, I got my Catering Apprenticeship Certificate with me. No need though. Tight jeans, queer chef? Sorted. Ahh! *(Cramp in his leg)*

He totters back onto the chaise longue.

STAN *grabs* **RONNIE**'s *bag and empties it on the chaise longue.*

What the fuck... You're violating my privacy. That's my property!

STAN *holds up a bag of Spice.*

STAN D'you mean this property? Spice. This is not a spliff in a disco. You can't afford this much. This is fuckin' dealin'. Remember what I said about cameras? No way do I take you to Blackpool with this in the car. We get stopped and I'm back in prison. Now you know. You can make your own way there. Watch out for patrol cars. Can you walk?

RONNIE S'only cramp. OK, Stan. I'm gonna be straight with you, the actual truth. The Spice. I found it in the toilet. Motorway services, that toilet remember? You should do. You should remember. I'm comin' out the cubicle and you're waving your dick at me. I'm thinkin' "How lucky's this?" Dick and dope together. But then you go for sleazy talkin' like "You'll know it when you get this up you". Like your some big shot porn star. Mister, you're family style! Family size! So don't fuckin' kid yourself!

STAN I didn't say that.

RONNIE If *you* didn't say it, you've got the only talking dick on the planet. I'm just sayin', Stan. I'm not a whore. "You'll know it when you get this up you?". To someone you don't know? No one ever said that to me.

STAN OK, I apologise. I got carried away. You did give me the glad eye.

RONNIE That don't make me a hooker.

STAN Jesus. What did I do wrong? You're walking out the men's room. I've got five seconds to connect. That's how it goes sometimes.

RONNIE Respect!

STAN I'm doing my best here. Will someone tell me which fuckin' opera this is!

RONNIE When you carried me upstairs did you undress me?

STAN *(beat, cough)* You've had your appendix out.

RONNIE Right. And did you...?

STAN No! I'm strictly consensual, and I'm not into comatose arses.

RONNIE *(cynical)* Yeah yeah, you've got more morals than Mary Poppins. So why was you in prison?

STAN Not now.

RONNIE I wanna know if I still like you or not?

STAN Grievous bodily harm.

RONNIE OK, that's cool.

STAN Satisfied? There's a homophobic asshole who's got a plastic jaw to remember me by. Come on, I'll drop you on the M6.

RONNIE M6? You said Blackpool, all the way.

STAN When did I say that?

RONNIE Last night, you said Blackpool.

STAN I can't risk it. Or maybe... Look, Ronnie, dump that stuff? I'll take my dad's suits to the charity shop. The Heart Foundation in Abingdon Street.

RONNIE Heart Foundation? You said he died of liver.

STAN When you die your heart stops.

Sound of a car. **STAN** *darts to the window to see who it is.*

Oh, shit. Evil Ivy. "Something wicked this way comes". *(Grabs the walking stick)* She's a witch. It's her broomstick in parking mode. She's come back for it.

RONNIE *(horrified)* You gonna smack her with that? She's old!

STAN I won't touch her. *(Brandishes the stick)* She's come back
for it. Actually, I could do with one of these for self defence.

STAN *goes out to answer the door.*

RONNIE If you live on your own, mate, get a dog! I would.
Two dogs!

Doorbell rings.

My Brindle'd rip their bollocks off.

End of Scene Two

Scene Three

STAN *and* IVY *(70s). She is wearing her outdoor coat and she keeps it on. She leans heavily on her walking stick.*

IVY Your dad got violent, did you know? So, the nurses stopped coming. Different ones every day, you never get to know them. Mostly foreign, which didn't go down well with your dad as you can imagine. They might have told us they'd backed off. We found him in a terrible mess. His tablet organizer all over the place. He didn't know what medication to take or when; daytime, night time. I phoned the office. I said you're lucky I haven't got a gun. Leaving a sick old man in that state!

STAN Is this what you've come for?

IVY Give me time, Stan. The hospice was a blessing. We were humbled.

STAN So humble Derrick decides to stay home.

IVY "Blessed are the meek for they shall inherit the Earth".

STAN Aye, well they all want to dominate the Earth nowadays, even the fuckin' meek. Sorry! Language.

Enter RONNIE, *ready to depart.*

RONNIE Stan, we've gotta go.

STAN Ivy, can it wait?

RONNIE I've texted Karl. He's not happy.

IVY *(to* RONNIE*)* Have we been introduced?

RONNIE What's she sayin'?

STAN *(perfunctory)* Ivy Ronnie, Ronnie Ivy. This is not a convenient time. Ronnie's got an appointment in Blackpool.

RONNIE *(to* IVY*)* I'm late.

IVY *(urgent, to* STAN*)* Listen, Derrick sent me. I've had a right talking to.

She takes the picture out of her bag.

He says it's rightfully yours. And the other things if you want them.

STAN Blimey, a good deed. I bet you'll regret it by tomorrow. *(Takes the picture)* Thank you anyway. I'm sorry I can't offer you a cuppa tea. No names mentioned, someone had us disconnected, didn't they?

Text message ping on RONNIE*'s phone. He reads it.*

IVY I've come to tell you about your father. Things you should be told. It won't take long, but it might upset you. I was going to write but Derrick insisted...

STAN Yea, before the police come for you?

IVY No. There's no ulterior motive. Stan, this isn't easy. We both want to go to our graves with a clear conscience.

STAN Well, I'm delighted for you. Why don't I come over to your place one afternoon?

RONNIE Stan! Karl's texted me!

STAN Ronnie, take it easy.

RONNIE He's postponed the interview an hour.

IVY *(to* RONNIE*)* Young man, patience is a virtue.

STAN He hasn't got any. Virtue. *(Winks at* RONNIE*)* He's a sinner like me.

RONNIE Not like you, mate. Stan, this is above and beyond the call of duty. Read it.

STAN There's no need to bring the rest back. This is all I want. You've done the right thing.

RONNIE Stan, in return for postponing, Karl's got to give the manager a... *(Whisper)* B/J!

IVY *looks at* STAN *none the wiser.*

STAN *(to* IVY*)* Just a joke. *(Turns to* RONNIE *and signals frantically to leave the room)*

RONNIE What about the traffic?

STAN We've time now.

RONNIE *(about to text)* What time do I say then?

STAN Quarter to.

RONNIE Safe.

RONNIE *leaves as he texts Karl. Exit.*

STAN Ivy, it's a job interview. It's important.

IVY *(not hearing him, looking around)* When I was a girl this room was as grand as a ballroom. My own ballroom. Dancing at Christmas. Your father encouraged dancing at Easter as well, to sell more drinks.

STAN Yes, we know. You in your fairy dress. Go on.

RONNIE *re-appears briefly, impatient for* STAN *to follow. Then he goes.*

IVY *(pause)* He didn't know us anymore. But I kept on talking to him. What the mind doesn't know, the heart still feels. Like the stars in the sky which disappear in daylight, but they're still there, aren't they? No doubt the end was aggravated by alcohol. Liver failure was a merciful short cut.

So, we *had* to close down the business, and all the various accounts. Some of the regulars stay in contact but... I suppose you'll sell. Some even remember your granddad who was a wonderful chef.

STAN Jesus Christ, his omelettes were as flat as a rubber mouse pad.

IVY May we not take the Lord's name in vain?

STAN I don't believe in God.

IVY We know that. I'm not trying to convert you.

STAN I believe in the Higgs Boson particle. You do a lot of reading inside or you zone out on drugs. Poor sods, can you blame them, incarcerated twenty-three hours a day? Spice is like a ride on a time machine. You can go anywhere from here to oblivion.

IVY So, what *is* this Higgs thing?

STAN Astro-physics. The Higgs Boson particle binds molecules together to form solid matter.

IVY Huh. That happens every time *I* make an omelette.

STAN It's how the world began. God didn't make the world.

IVY Who made the molecules?

STAN *(beat. He can't answer)* You said you had something *important* to tell me.

IVY Highly personal.

STAN I'm not being rude, but there's no time now.

IVY The boy's gone. I've just seen him running down the drive. Let him go.

STAN *rushes to the window.*

Let him go!

STAN I'll go after him. He's not in a good way.

IVY Who is he?

STAN He's just a friend.

IVY Oh, *that* sort of friend? Stan, you're a fool to yourself, chasing after boys. Oh, we all know.

STAN I promised him a ride to Blackpool.

IVY *(cynical)* Yes, yes, yes.

STAN   He wants to go on the Pleasure Beach. Mad about rollercoasters.

IVY   Think what you're doing, apart from making a fool of yourself. You're too old for him. Derrick and I are not strangers to the world—or *your* world. We don't mention it, of course we don't. We're not part of it. Disappearing at night, d'you think we don't know what for? *(Beat)* What y'doin' standin' there for? Sit down and listen. Despite the absence of any formal will...

STAN   Are you sure?

IVY   We've turned the house upside down.

STAN   I can see that.

IVY   But... I have concrete evidence that this property does belong to you. That surprises you, doesn't it? So, get your priorities right, Stan. Let the boy go. Resist temptation. That's all it is, temptation. Boys like him are ten a penny.

STAN   I like him.

IVY   *(quietly)* I know you do. I liked someone once.

STAN   The six-foot six brickie?

IVY   Talk to anyone, Stan. There's always the one that got away. *(Pause)* Sit down.

> STAN *is unsettled. He wants to leave, but in the end, he sits down to quietly listen.*

Your dad's ashes are laid in the Glade of Remembrance.

STAN   Is that it?

IVY   You'd know that if you'd been there.

STAN   I couldn't get day release.

IVY   Not even for a close relation?

STAN   You don't mess with the screws. Nazi swine. I spat in the bastard's face. So, while he's choking me he says "Think yourself lucky homo. In other countries people like you are lined up against a wall and shot". He meant it an' all. It got me twenty-one days solitary. Nearest thing to buried alive. *(Beat)* I've had enough.

IVY People want too much out of life. They want everything all the time. D'you know why? I blame television. They see everything, they want everything, and when they don't get it... Pray for deliverance from evil. *(Wags her finger)* You can't pray to a molecule.

STAN You can pray to a bloody grapefruit, Ivy. What matters is where it gets you.

IVY *sits down, wearily in pain.*

IVY If you say so.

STAN What good's it done *you*?

IVY It gives me the strength I need. The new medicine doesn't kill the pain. It only helps to bear the pain. Stan, don't question people's faith. If they're not hurting you.

STAN There's many who would. This evidence you've got, is it in writing?

IVY Yes.

STAN Can I see it?

IVY Stan, bear with me. Don't get angry like you usually do. Life isn't always in a straight line. Things happen. Things go wrong. When they do... Are you listening? What Derrick said as I was leaving. There is such a thing as forgiveness.

STAN Is there? It's takes time, though. How long have I been...

IVY Not just you! All of us. There's always someone to forgive.

STAN I love mystery stories, Ivy, but not now. This is not Poirot.

IVY Like y'dad and you. The care home was a nightmare. The council kept asking who's going to pay. Not you, locked up.

And we couldn't afford fifteen thousand pounds a month.
Finally, we got him into a hospice. Our Lady, Star of the
Sea with a beautiful garden.

STAN　Who have I got to forgive?

IVY　Your dad died peacefully in his sleep. But there was
something strange. On the way in we met the mother
superior. She had a beautiful speaking voice like an oboe.
She came forward and graciously informed us that your
dad had seen the angels. He was preparing to depart this
life. It might be at dawn. Or the next day. They know these
things. So, we waited. Through the night they brought us
cups of tea.

She now addresses STAN *directly.*

Around midnight he began to talk in a foreign language.
That's what it sounded like to me. But he never spoke any
foreign languages in his life, did he? You know what he
was like. He thought the Isle of Man was a foreign country.
Anyway, it was no language I know. He was delirious, so
we didn't think much of it. But then he suddenly stopped
talking gibberish. He sat up straight in bed and shouted.
"Send Stan the letter"! I nearly passed out on the spot.

STAN　What letter?

IVY　*(with difficulty)* I never posted it. I tore it up. How did he
know? Was he in touch with a higher power?

STAN　No, forget the higher power. He was expecting me to
reply. It doesn't take a higher power to work that out.

IVY　Don't worry. Unbeknown to me, Derrick's kept it. He's just
given it to me.

She opens her bag and gives STAN *a letter which has
been torn and sellotaped.*

It makes no material difference. You're next of kin anyway.
It's not a crime, Stan, but Derrick said we should expiate
our sins and make our peace.

STAN Your getaway man?

IVY Read the letter. Your father gives us leave to take something to remember him by.

STAN Remember him by? You went to fuckin' town.

IVY *(she flinches at the bad language)* We assumed you'd sell everything. That's nothing to remember him by, some second-hand shop'd get it all for a few pounds. Admit it, Stan. You want the money. You're not married. There'll never be any kids. We had good intentions, but you always think the worst of everyone. You've been like it all your life.

STAN *gets up and looks out of the window.*

Rain. I don't like driving in the rain. You didn't want that boy to hear all this, did you?

STAN *reads the letter. He nearly cries.*

STAN This is from the heart, a father's love.

IVY That's why I plead forgiveness. It's always best to do the right thing in the end.

STAN My father's last words to me.

IVY There was something else. He said: "Tell Stan I didn't mean it". I can't explain that one. He was rambling.

STAN I can. The runt in a litter of one.

IVY Right at the end. He rallied like they sometimes do. "Open the curtains", he ordered, in his usual gruff way. Again, we waited in silence, a silence so profound I knew something transcendent was about to happen. His hair was spread across the pillow, shining golden in the sunlight. His face, radiant with happiness, seemed young and alive. From all corners of the room we heard whispering sounds in that strange language, words floating in the air like prayers you could breathe in. It was no language of this world. It was the angels. When the time came, his spirit rose out of his body like a mist... And last of all: a sweet scent of roses,

roses in a summer garden. *(She exits)* If I see the boy on the road, shall I stop for him?

STAN What, you?

She's gone.

End of Scene Three

Scene Four

A Thunderstorm Rages

RONNIE *is seated wearing a bath towel round his shoulders. His bag is by his side. He rummages for a clean pair of jeans and another t-shirt. He's already put clean shorts on.*

IVY *enters carrying a bag of shopping.*

IVY This bag's been nowhere near the kitchen. You won't get dysentery. Six cans of Coca-Cola. That should keep y'goin'.

She takes out a six pack of Coca-Cola and struggles to open it.

RONNIE *goes over to help her.*

I'll leave them there. Don't let Stan put them in the kitchen. He's daft enough. Put some in your bag.

RONNIE D'you think *I'm* daft?

IVY You're all daft. Did you fasten the window?

RONNIE It's broken.

She looks at the window to see if **STAN** *is coming home.*

RONNIE *opens a can of Coke and drinks.*

IVY You know what he's like. He worked in security. That didn't suit him. Before that... How much has he told you?

RONNIE He's got a bad temper.

IVY You can say that again, and the language. He doesn't care who it is gets an earful. Lost one job after another telling his bosses where to go.

RONNIE I do that.

IVY He's his own worst enemy. Now, are you going to be all right? Remember what to say: you were drowning out there and I brought you back.

RONNIE He might buy some candles. I hope so.

IVY He's looking for *you*. He won't go far. He knows on the motorway you're soon on your way.

RONNIE I'm supposed to be in Blackpool. I've missed my interview, the manager of the hotel. Stan's got all these issues, one thing after another. Is this what I left home for?

IVY *(knowing)* He doesn't want you to go.

RONNIE Keepin' me prisoner?

IVY Stan wears his heart on his sleeve, and not just his heart, but we won't go there. You're not a prisoner. You're free to go, aren't you? *(Beat)* My husband's waiting for me.

She heads for the door.

RONNIE Thanks for the lift... and the Coke.

IVY *stops and turns round.*

IVY You're in catering, aren't you?

RONNIE Yeah, lookin' for a job.

IVY What d'you think of this place? It was the finest guest house in the area. Regulars every year. But after Stan's mother died his father...

A door slams off.

STAN *enters with more shopping.*

STAN *(cheerful)* Eh, look who's here then safe and sound! I've been lookin' all over. Where did you find 'im?

IVY Bedraggled under a tree.

STAN I've been looking for you. I got as far as the motorway. *(Takes bottles of water out of the shopping bag)* Water.

Candles. I remembered what you said about our water. I thought you'd gone but I bought it all the same. Funny how the mind works.

IVY Funny how it doesn't.

STAN I bet you're gagging for a drink.

IVY Have you gone blind? He's got one.

STAN I assure you this is not aquarium water. Paid good money for it against my principles but... Only sparkling, I'm afraid. Don't you know bottled water sits in warehouses for weeks? People don't realise. You tell 'im Ivy. Our water is fresh from a mountain spring.

IVY The pipes are rusty.

STAN Thanks for that.

RONNIE They're buying up the water supply. Big business. The reservoirs and lakes.

IVY They can't buy the rain clouds.

STAN *(snaps fingers)* Nice one.

IVY *turns to go and moves slowly towards the door using her stick.*

A sidelight goes on. The same one STAN *tried in Scene One.*

We're re-connected!

IVY Derrick said he'd get onto them.

STAN They wouldn't do it for *me*.

IVY You were rude to them I'm sure. How many times have you cut your nose to spite your face? When your dad took his belt to you, that's when you behaved yourself; for a short while until he'd thrash you again.

STAN I'll ignore these remarks for the sake of goodwill. You did us all a good turn today, Ivy. Welcome back to humanity. We'll savour the moment. *(To* **RONNIE***)* I take it the job's not on?

RONNIE Karl's blocked me.

STAN Was it ever really on? This Karl character sounds decidedly flaky.

IVY *(going)* The lad's hungry. He's had a Snicker bar, that's all. Did *you* get anything?

STAN He won't touch it.

IVY Derrick's wants his tea an' all.

IVY starts a slow silent exit.

STAN We'll have to go out. How about a cheese burger, onion rings, chicken nuggets, double fries? You can overdose on vitamin Z.

RONNIE Yes please, where?

STAN Motorway services. Or fish and chips in Blackpool? Rollercoaster rides thrown in. My treat. You can eat after the rollercoaster though, not before. What d'you say?

RONNIE *(excited)* It's Firework Night.

STAN *(sharing his excitement)* I know. You told me. And then we'll come back here. You've nowhere else to stay. *(Beat)* If you want to, that is.

RONNIE What's happened? Have you won the lottery?

STAN *(pauses. He takes the sellotaped letter from his pocket)* My dad's forgiven me.

RONNIE What for?

STAN Dealin'. *(Beat)* Now you know. Next time it's five years.

The front door slams shut. They now see that **IVY** *has gone.*

What did you do with the drugs?

RONNIE Dumped 'em in a field.

STAN Are you serious? The cows are jumpin' over the moon, Mars and fuckin' Jupiter. Are you telling more lies?

RONNIE The rain washed it away.

STAN What about the bag it was in?

RONNIE What about it? No one'll find it. Stan, the old girl said I can stay here tonight.

STAN Oh, she did, did she? It's not for her to say. I suppose you'll have to. It just better be true that you fed the drugs to the cows.

STAN sits on the chaise longue.

RONNIE Is it true you broke a guy's jaw?

STAN Why d'you ask?

RONNIE That homophobe? You smacked him and now he's got a plastic jawbone?

STAN Yeah. *(He's lying)* It sounded like a stick snapping. Knocked him down the iron steps while his teeth were falling out. A burst artery, blood everywhere. One eye hanging out. I ran down the steps three at a time and jumped on him. They had to drag me off or he'd be dead.

RONNIE sits on the chaise longue by STAN's side.

RONNIE *(knowingly)* Too much detail mate.

They lie back on the chaise longue.

Silence, then...

STAN There's no obligation.

RONNIE What's that mean?

STAN You know. No obligation if you stay. Plenty of clean bedding in the linen cupboard. Hot water's back on. I dunno what tea's like made with San Pellegrino, but I'll try anything once. *(Beat)* Tell me something, Ronnie. Am I too old?

RONNIE I quite like older. Straight looking in a suit. Pinstripe. I don't like zombies either. Zombies don't wear pinstripe suits.

STAN I'm sure a few million business wives don't agree with you. A couple of things struck me that Ivy said. On his deathbed my dad saw the angels.

RONNIE Saw the angels?

STAN It means you're fucked. Then the stars; they disappear in daylight, but they're still there. That got to me.

RONNIE You could say that about quite a few things, which are invisible.

STAN Such as?

RONNIE Where d'you start? This house? It was a hotel, wasn't it?

STAN Guest house.

RONNIE Are you gonna do it up?

STAN One way or another, sell up or stay, it needs work.

RONNIE You could open a queer guest house.

STAN You can't turn straights away. It's against the law.

RONNIE If there's a gap in the market though... There's queer bird watching, cycling, hill climbing... And if you run a good kitchen... We did cash flow at college. A guest lecturer came who was big on bulding a business reputation. All the value is in the goodwill.

STAN Clever little bugger on the quiet, aren't you? Tell me summat. What's the difference between a queer hotel and a straight one?

RONNIE Candlelight breakfast. It's what I'd do anyway. You're lucky. I wish my dad'd die and leave me a house.

STAN Sounds suspiciously like you're talking your way into a job.

RONNIE Oh, and get a dog.

STAN Two dogs you said.

RONNIE Yeah, two dogs.

STAN *(tentative)* Or I get a Mastiff, then what say you and me drive to London to fetch Brindle? Just imaginin' things like y'know.

RONNIE It's your Aunty Ivy's idea. She wants you to settle down and re-open the business. Start with the kitchen. Clean that up. Then all the bathrooms. Redecorate, landscape the garden...

STAN I'm in a cold sweat 'ere, hot flushes and palpitations.

RONNIE You're right. She's a witch.

RONNIE snuggles up to STAN. STAN slowly puts his arm round RONNIE.

A rollercoaster and fireworks take us to THE END.

PROPS

A painting of a passenger boat on Lake Windermere
A glass of water. (Scene 1)
A table or standard lamp
A rucksack for Ronnie
A holdall for Ivy
Folding steps
Walking stick
A sachet of drugs (Spice)
Bottles of water and/or Coca-Cola
Three bags of shopping. Two in Scene 1. One in Scene 4
Walking stick
Painting
Set of keys
A granny-bag pull along full of knick-knacks and antiques
Mobile phone (Stan)
Mobile phone (Ronnie)
A glass of water
Letter for Stan from his dad that has been torn and sellotaped
Handbag for Ivy
A bath towel
Bag for Ronnie (rucksack)
Bag of shopping for Ivy
Six pack cans of Coca Cola
Can of coke for Ronnie to drink
More shopping bags for Stan
Bottle of water in the shopping bags
Candles in the shopping bags

THIS
IS
NOT
THE
END

**Visit samuelfrench.co.uk
and discover the best
theatre bookshop
on the internet.**

A vast range of plays
Acting and theatre books
Gifts

samuelfrench.co.uk

samuelfrenchltd

samuel french uk

Lightning Source UK Ltd.
Milton Keynes UK
UKHW02f0050020918
328164UK00006B/170/P